THE STORY OF CHRISTMAS

A Picture Book by Felix Hoffmann

Atheneum · New York

A MARGARET K. MCELDERRY BOOK

Library of Congress catalog card number: 75–6921   ISBN 0–689–50031–9

NEARLY TWO THOUSAND YEARS AGO there lived in Nazareth, a little town in Judea, a girl named Mary who was to marry Joseph, a carpenter.

One day, the Angel Gabriel appeared before her and said, "Fear not, Mary, for you have found favor with God. You will have a son and you shall name him Jesus. This child will become the saviour of all mankind."

At this time, the Roman Emperor Caesar Augustus, who ruled over many lands, wanted to find out how many people were living in his empire so that he could tax them. He sent forth a proclamation that everyone must go to the place where he had been born to be counted and recorded.

Joseph, the carpenter, came from the city of Bethlehem so, according to the Emperor's command, he started with his wife Mary on the long journey to his birthplace.

Since Mary was expecting her child, they traveled very slowly. When they finally came to the city's gate, Bethlehem was crowded with people and there was no room for them to stay in any inn or house. It was late in the evening before they found a place to rest—in a small stable.

During that night, Mary gave birth to a son. She wrapped him in swaddling clothes and laid him in a manger for his crib.

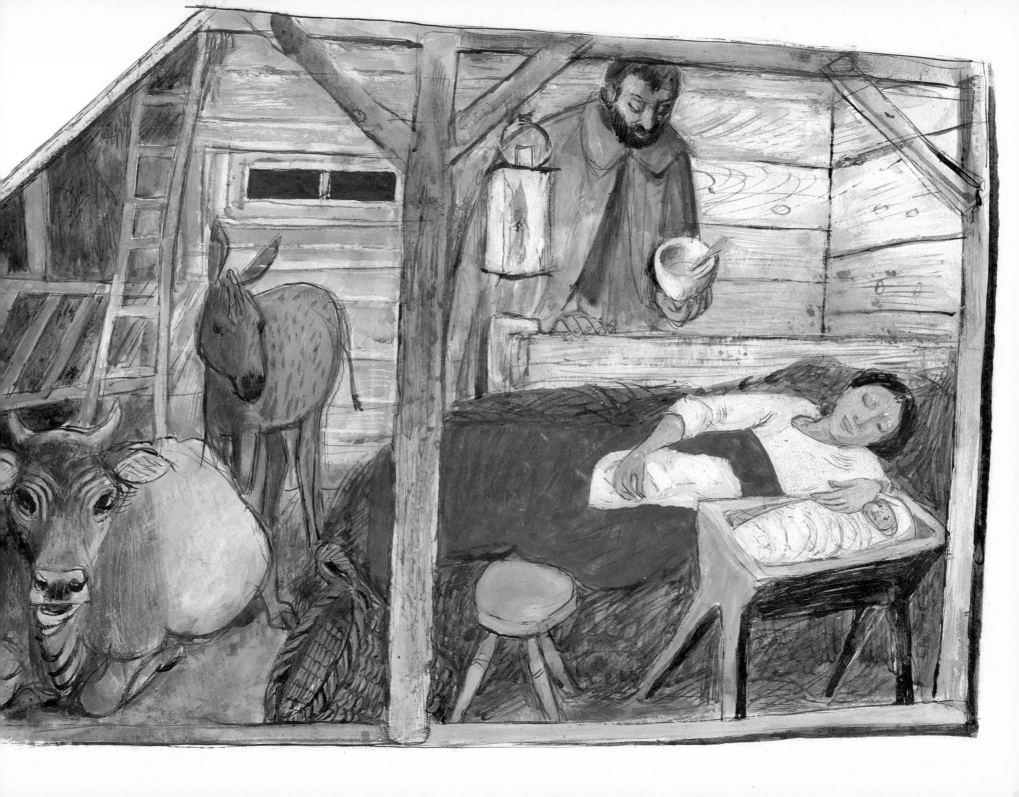

On that same night, some shepherds were keeping watch over their flocks in the field.

Suddenly, the Angel of the Lord appeared to them. A wondrous light, as bright as day, shone around them. And they were sore afraid. The Angel spoke: "Fear not! For behold, I bring you good tidings of great joy—to you and all mankind. Tonight, the saviour of the world is born. Go to Bethlehem, where you will find the newborn babe, lying in a manger."

And lo, a great host of angels came and sang: "Glory to God in the highest and on earth peace and good will toward all men."

After the angels left, the night was as dark as before. For a long time the shepherds were silent. Then they spoke to each other. "Let us go to Bethlehem and see if what the Angel told us is true." And they left their flocks.

They found the stable and saw Joseph and Mary, and the child was lying in the manger. Then they knew that all the Angel had told them was indeed true, and they rejoiced.

When the shepherds left the stable, they praised the Lord for everything they had seen, and they spread the news far and wide among the people.

Mary remembered all the glorious things she had heard and treasured them in her heart.

Now it happened that three wise men from the East, who understood the meaning of the stars, came to Jerusalem. They asked, "Where is the newborn babe who one day will be the saviour of mankind? In our homeland, we saw a huge star, rising in the sky, that told us of his birth. We followed the star, but now we have lost it."

No one could give them an answer.

When Herod, who was King of Judea, heard about the child, he was troubled for he feared he would no longer be king after the child had grown up. He invited the three wise men from the East to his palace and asked them to search for the child and let him know when they found it, so that he, too, might go and worship.

As they were leaving the King's palace, the wise men saw the star again. Overjoyed, they followed it once more. The star went before them until it stopped over the small stable.

The wise men entered and found the child with his mother Mary. They knelt before it and worshipped it. Then they unwrapped their gifts and gave the baby incense, myrrh, and gold.

That night, the three wise men all had the same dream. An angel told them not to reveal to King Herod where they had found the child, because he planned an evil deed. So they returned to their homeland by a different road.

On that same night, the Angel of the Lord appeared also to Joseph in a dream and spoke. "Take the child and his mother at once and flee into Egypt. Stay there until I bring you word, because Herod plans to kill the child Jesus." Joseph woke up, told his dream to Mary, and they began their long flight into Egypt.

When King Herod found out that the three wise men from
the East had not returned to tell him what they had dis-
covered, he was enraged and fearful. He sent his soldiers
to Bethlehem to kill all the baby boys there who were
under two years of age.

Joseph and Mary stayed in Egypt with the child Jesus until
the angel of the Lord told them of King Herod's death.

Then they returned to Nazareth where the boy Jesus grew up.